GW00739177

VICTORIA AVENUE PAPER COMPANY

A division of
The Five Mile Press Pty Ltd
67 Rushdale Street
Knoxfield Victoria 3180

First published 1993

Compiled by Maggie Pinkney
Designed by SBR Productions
Production: Emma Borghesi
Printed in Singapore

National Library of Australia
Cataloguing-in-Publication data

Reflections on friendship

ISBN 0 86788 545 9

1. Friendship - Poetry.
2. Friendship - Quotations, maxims, etc.

808.819353

Reflections on Friendship

AN ANTHOLOGY OF SPECIAL THOUGHTS

Illustrated by Margie Chellew

Victoria Avenue
PAPER COMPANY

True Friendship

A real friend is one who walks
in when the rest of the world
walks out.

Walter Winchell 1879–1972

To like and dislike the same things,
that is indeed true friendship.

Sallust c.86–34BC

A friend is someone with whom I may be sincere. Before him I may think aloud.

Ralph Waldo Emerson 1803–1882

True friendship is a plant of slow growth and must undergo and withstand the shocks of adversity before it is entitled to the appellation.

George Washington 1732–1799

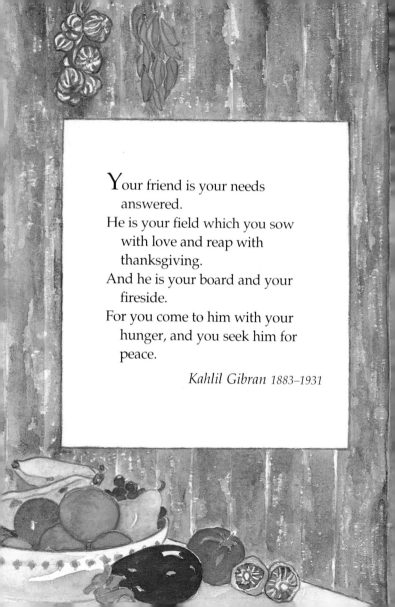

Your friend is your needs answered.

He is your field which you sow with love and reap with thanksgiving.

And he is your board and your fireside.

For you come to him with your hunger, and you seek him for peace.

Kahlil Gibran 1883–1931

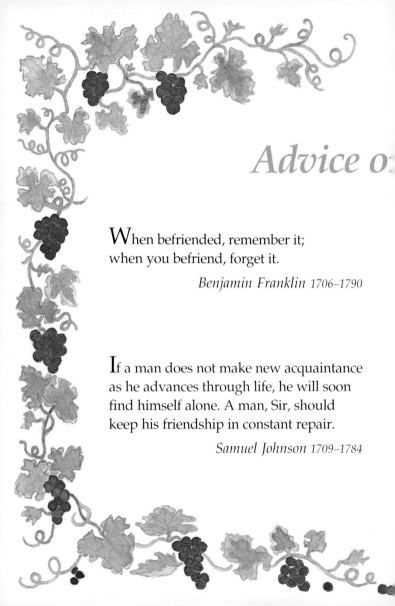

Advice o

When befriended, remember it;
when you befriend, forget it.

Benjamin Franklin 1706–1790

If a man does not make new acquaintance
as he advances through life, he will soon
find himself alone. A man, Sir, should
keep his friendship in constant repair.

Samuel Johnson 1709–1784

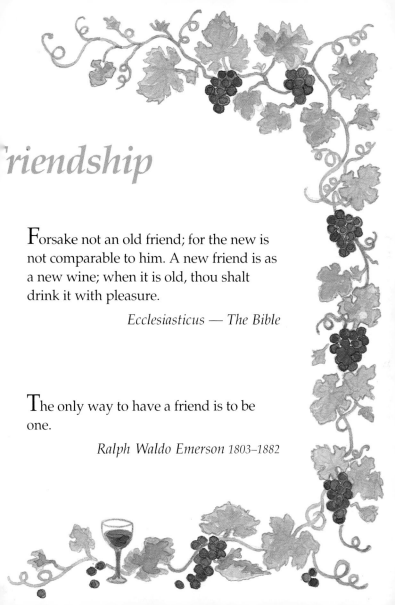

riendship

Forsake not an old friend; for the new is
not comparable to him. A new friend is as
a new wine; when it is old, thou shalt
drink it with pleasure.

Ecclesiasticus — The Bible

The only way to have a friend is to be
one.

Ralph Waldo Emerson 1803–1882

From a letter...

I like not only to be loved but also
to be told I am loved. The realm of
silence is large enough beyond the
grave. This is the world of light and
speech. And I shall take leave to tell
you that you are very dear.

George Eliot 1819–1880

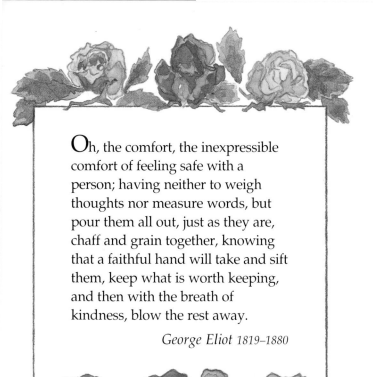

Oh, the comfort, the inexpressible comfort of feeling safe with a person; having neither to weigh thoughts nor measure words, but pour them all out, just as they are, chaff and grain together, knowing that a faithful hand will take and sift them, keep what is worth keeping, and then with the breath of kindness, blow the rest away.

George Eliot 1819–1880

On Friendship

Let there be no purpose in friendship
save the deepening of the spirit.
For love that seeks aught but the disclosure
of its own mystery is not love but a net cast
forth: and only the unprofitable is caught.

And let your best be for your friend.
If he must know the ebb of your tide, let him
know its flood also.
For what is your friend that you should seek
him with hours to kill?
Seek him always with hours to live.
For it is his to fill your need, but not your
emptiness.

And in the sweetness of friendship let there be laughter, and sharing of pleasures. For in the dew of little things the heart finds its morning and is refreshed.

Kahlil Gibran 1883–1931

Reflections

Fate chooses your relations, you choose your friends.

Jacques Delille 1738–1813

If you have a friend worth loving
Love him. Yes, and let him know
That you love him, ere life's evening
Tinge his brow with sunset glow.
Why should good words ne'er be
said
Of a friend till he is dead?

Daniel W. Hoyt

Animals are such agreeable friends — they ask no questions, they pass no criticisms.

George Eliot 1819–1880

Friendship is almost always the union of a part of one mind with a part of another; people are friends in spots.

George Santayana 1863–1952

I always felt that the great high privilege, relief and comfort of friendship was that one had to explain nothing.

Katherine Mansfield 1888–1923

Friendship

It is fit for serene days,
and graceful gifts and country
rambles, but also for rough roads
and hard fare, shipwreck, poverty
and persecution... It should never
fall into something usual and
settled, but should be alert and
inventive, and add rhyme
and reason to what was
drudgery.

Ralph Waldo Emerson
1803–1882

A FRIEND is someone who's always on your side — even when you're in the wrong.

A FRIEND is someone who has your kids to stay over when you have the flu.

A FRIEND is someone who says you look great when you've just had a radical haircut.

A FRIEND is someone who brings the dessert when you're giving an important dinner party.

A FRIEND is someone who says the 'other woman' is a total bimbo.

A FRIEND doesn't always let you win when you insist on picking up the bill after a meal out.

Natalie Nicholls

That's What Friends Are For ...

What do we live for, if it is not to make life less difficult for each other?

George Eliot 1819–1880

There is only one task, and that is to increase the store of love within us.

Leo Tolstoy 1828–1910

People must help one another; it is nature's law.

Jean de La Fontaine 1621–1695

Life is mostly froth and bubble.
Two things stand like stone.
Kindness in another's trouble,
Courage in your own.

Adam Lindsay Gordon 1833–1879

Love is blind. Friendship closes its eyes.

Anon.

A hedge between keeps friendship green.

Anon.

A different taste in jokes is a great strain on the affections.

George Eliot 1818–1880

A friend in need is a friend indeed.

Anon.

Misfortune teaches us who our real friends are.

Anon.

Friendship is tested in the thick years of success rather than in the thin years of struggle.

Barry Humphries

Books as Friends

A good book is the best of friends, the same today and for ever.

Martin Farquhar Tupper 1810–1889

The first time I read an excellent book, it is to me just as if I have gained a new friend; when I read over a book I have perused before, it resembles the meeting with an old one.

Oliver Goldsmith 1728–1774

Life's Rewards

An elegant sufficiency,
Retirement, rural quiet, friendship, books.

James Thomson 1700–1748

Thoughts for a Friend

When you arise in the morning
Give thanks for the morning light.
Give thanks for your life and strength.
Give thanks for your food.
And give thanks for the joy of living.
And if perchance you see no reason
For giving thanks,
Rest assured the fault is in yourself.

North American Indian saying

Deep peace of the Running
   Wave to you.
Deep peace of the Flowing
   Air to you.
Deep peace of the Quiet Earth
   to you.
Deep peace of the Shining
   Stars to you.
Deep peace of the Son of
   Peace to you.

Celtic benediction